A New True Book

WOLVES

By Emilie U. Lepthien

CHILDRENS PRESS®
CHICAGO

A gray wolf

PHOTO CREDITS

© Alan & Sandy Carey—Cover, 15, 17, 24, 30, 33 (left), 40 (top)

Odyssey/Frerck/Chicago—© Robert Frerck, 43

Point Defiance Zoo & Aquarium—© Mel Woods, 37 (2 photos)

© Chris Roberts—10; © Wm. Munoz, 14, 26

© H. Armstrong Roberts—© Leonard Lee Rue III, 28

© San Diego Zoo—6 (bottom); © Ron Garrison, 5

Tom Stack & Associates—© Thomas Kitchin, 4 (top & bottom left), 21, 42; © Joe McDonald, 4 (bottom right); © Gary Milburn, 6 (top), 39; © Bill Everitt, 8; © Tom Stack, 13 (right), 35; © John Cancalosi, 27 (left)

© Lynn M. Stone—2, 9, 23, 27 (right), 33 (right), 40 (bottom), 44

TSW-CLICK/Chicago—© Leonard Lee Rue III, 13 (left); © Gary Bumgarner, 16

Valan—© Murray O'Niell, 11 (left & right); © Stephen J. Krasemann, 11 (center), 18, 36 (2 photos), 45; © Bob Gurr, 29 (left); © Bob Hyland

Cover: Gray wolves

To Ernelle and Otto Geyler

Library of Congress Cataloging-in-Publication Data

Lepthien, Emilie U. (Emilie Utteg)
    Wolves / by Emilie U. Lepthien.
        p.   cm. — (A New true book)
    Includes index.
    Summary: Describes the characteristics and
behavior of wolves and their relationship with humanity.
    ISBN 0-516-01129-4
    1. Wolves—Juvenile literature. [1. Wolves.]
I. Title.
QL737.C22L485   1991   91-3035
962—dc20   CIP
                                        AC

TABLE OF CONTENTS

Wolves (above) are related to coyotes (bottom left) and jackals (bottom right).

A wolf
mother and
her pups
in China

WHAT IS A WOLF?

A wolf is a member of a group of animals called mammals. Mammals have hair on their bodies and feed their young with milk.

Wolves are meat-eaters, or carnivores. They hunt other animals for food.

Wolves are related to jackals, coyotes, and dogs.

5

The gray wolf (above) is also called the timber wolf. The
tundra wolf (below) is a gray wolf that lives in the far north.

WHERE DO WOLVES LIVE?

Wolves once hunted across much of Asia and eastern and northern Europe. They lived in all parts of North America, and along the coast of Greenland.

The gray wolf, or timber wolf, was the most common wolf in the eastern United States and in Canada and Alaska.

Tundra wolves are gray

A Mexican wolf

wolves. They live in the far north and are larger than the wolves that live in Canada and in Minnesota.

The Mexican wolf is a smaller species than the gray wolf. It lives in the southwestern United

States and northern Mexico.
Another smaller species,
the red wolf, hunted from
the pine forests of east
Texas to the Atlantic. They
were found along the
Mississippi River Valley as
far north as central Illinois
and Indiana.

A red wolf

A wolf family group

THE WOLF PACK

Some wolves hunt alone.
Others hunt in pairs. But
most wolves hunt in packs.
A pack may be a family—
parents and offspring. If

game is plentiful, a pack
may have two or more
families.

The pack is important in
hunting. Working together,
the wolves chase and
surround their prey. Wolves
hunt deer, elk, moose,
caribou, beaver, and

Wolves hunt deer (left),
moose (above),
and caribou (right).

rabbits and other small animals. Generally, wolves catch old, sick, or injured animals and the very young. Wolves can go without eating for three or four days.

Wolves mark their territories with their scent. Each pack may cover a territory of 50 square miles. They prefer woods bordering on open areas.

Wolves live in groups called packs. The wolf at left is checking out a scent mark on a tree.

Wolves are social animals. To survive they must work together. Different pack members may take charge during travel, hunting, feeding, and guarding the territory. **13**

The alpha male is usually the biggest and strongest wolf.

The leading male of the pack is called the alpha male. Other members of the pack recognize his leadership. The alpha female is the most important female. Usually she will mate with the alpha male.

Wolf pups in their den

WOLF PUPS

Before the pups are born,
the mother digs a den or
finds a cave for them. Pups
are born in March or April.
There may be four to six
pups in a litter.

Newborn pups are blind
and deaf. After a few days

15

A young wolf pup goes exploring outside the den.

they can hear. In about
two weeks they open their
eyes. Their floppy ears will
stand up after a month.
Over half of the pups do
not survive.

Young wolves learn from older pack members.

After the pups are weaned, other members of the pack will help to feed them. They will play with them and teach them to hunt.

17

WOLVES AND PEOPLE

The original range of
wolves in North America
decreased as people moved
in and built towns. The farmers
and ranchers were afraid
wolves would attack their
animals. So wolves were
hunted and killed.

The colonists of Jamestown, Virginia, brought cattle, horses, and pigs with them. The colonists knew wolves in Europe. To protect their animals, they dug wolf pits and built fences. They also hired hunters. Bounty laws were passed in Massachusetts in 1630 and in Jamestown in 1632. Native Americans were paid for wolf pelts with blankets and trinkets. Later, other states passed bounty laws too. The gray wolf disappeared from all of the lower 48 states except Minnesota.

Wolves in Europe faced a similar fate. Today there are no wolves in Great Britain and Scandinavia. Only a small number remain in other parts of Europe.

In Canada and Alaska there are between 20,000 and 25,000 gray wolves. Minnesota has between 1,000 and 1,200.

Gray wolf or timber wolf

WOLF ANCESTORS

Ancestors of the wolf developed millions of years ago. One million years ago, Canis, the immediate ancestor of the wolf, appeared. It had a

21

longer nose and a larger brain than earlier members of the family. Longer, strong legs helped it run faster. These animals hunted in small groups. They were probably the ancestors of the dog as well.

SIZE OF WOLVES

The size of wolves depends on where they live. In warmer regions, they weigh about 45 pounds. In Alaska they may weigh 100 or more pounds. Female wolves

Arctic wolf or white wolf

Wolves learn how to behave in the pack when they play. The male is showing his higher rank by standing. The female shows her acceptance of his power by lying down with her ears back.

weigh several pounds less than males.

They measure about 3 to 4½ feet in length. Their thickly furred tail is half as long. They stand about 31 inches tall at the shoulder.

A LUXURIOUS COAT

The gray wolf varies in color from almost white to cream, gray, brown, or black.

Its coat has two layers. Long guard hairs cover a soft, dense underfur. The guard hairs keep the underfur dry. In spring, wolves shed much of their underfur and some guard hairs. The fur grows back before winter.

The guard hairs on their
legs and muzzle are thin.
In cold weather, wolves
tuck their muzzles and
noses between their hind
legs when they lie down.
They cover their faces with
their thick, furry tails.

A Mexican gray wolf (left) with pointed ears. An arctic wolf (above) with rounded ears.

ADAPTATIONS TO CLIMATE

Gray wolves in warmer climates have large, pointed ears. Those in the tundra regions have short, rounded ears. Large ears help to give off body heat. Short ears help the wolf withstand cold weather better.

When wolves pant, they also give off body heat. In hot weather, they may hunt during the cool hours of the night.

Wolves pant to keep cool.

COMMUNICATION AND HEARING

Wolves communicate through their body positions. A wolf standing with its tail up and its ears pointed forward is showing power. A wolf crouching with its tail between its legs and its ears turned down is showing

Howling is another way of communicating.

that it has less power in the
pack than the standing wolf.
By howling, wolves
assemble the pack. They
howl to find each other in
a storm. Their howls warn
of danger. Wolves do not

howl at the moon. When several wolves howl together, they harmonize.

Wolves rarely bark. A quiet "woof" might be heard when the pack is surprised at a den. Unlike dogs, they do not bark continually. Pups growl while playing. Their parents squeak when the pups' play is too rough.

Wolves have very good hearing. They can hear mice scurrying under the snow. They can hear sounds that are higher-pitched than we can hear.

They also have a keen sense of smell. They can pick up the odor of another animal a mile away. Wolves warn strange wolves to stay out of their territory by leaving scent marks.

Wolves have strong jaws and teeth. They have sharp fangs called canines that can cut and tear flesh. Usually they do not kill more than they can eat.

Wolf chews on a moose antler (left). Wolf pack eating a deer (right)

THE ENDANGERED SPECIES ACT

In 1973 the United States passed the Endangered Species Act. The act was passed to protect animals threatened with extinction. It protected wolves in every state except Alaska and Minnesota. Wolves were considered "threatened," rather than endangered, in Minnesota.

In 1982 the act was amended so that problem wolves could be killed legally. Farmers would be paid for cattle they could prove were killed by wolves.

Each year, between 35 and 45 wolves are killed legally as predators in

The pelt of
a gray wolf

Minnesota. Several hundred are killed illegally for their valuable coats.

The larger, heavier pelts of the Alaskan and Canadian tundra wolves bring a higher price than those of gray wolves.

WOLF RECOVERY PROGRAMS

In 1980 the red wolf
was declared nearly
extinct in the wild. Only a
few lived in coastal
marshes in Texas and

A red wolf from a recovery program in North Carolina is released in the wild.

A red wolf adult and pup in the Point Defiance Zoological Park

Louisiana. Scientists found that red wolves had mated with coyotes. There were only 14 pure red wolves at the Point Defiance Zoological Park in Tacoma, Washington.

Today there are 16 different Red Wolf Recovery Programs. Under these programs, red wolves are born in captivity and later released. Only about 40 percent of these wolves survive in the wild. There are now about 109 red wolves living in the wild and in captivity.

The Mexican wolf lived in a desert habitat. It hunted rabbits and other small animals.

Scientists are trying to save the Mexican wolf.

In 1942 it was declared extinct in the United States. A few were found, however. Now 39 Mexican wolves exist in captive breeding programs.

Yellowstone National Park (below) has many elk for wolves to hunt.

THE WOLF'S FUTURE

The U.S. Fish and Wildlife Service has approved a program to reintroduce the gray wolf in the northern Rockies. Ten breeding pairs of gray wolves would be released in Glacier National Park, in the wilderness of central Idaho, and in Yellowstone National Park and adjoining areas.

Wolves kill sick and injured animals. This helps keep the herds healthy.

Various government agencies are studying the proposal. They must agree on the best way to manage the wolves.

When Yellowstone National Park was established in 1872, the

This bison seems to have its hunter on the run.

wolf was the only native species that was missing. The wolves had all been killed. Biologists say this recovery program is good. Wolves would restore the natural balance of the elk and bison in the area.

But hunters and trappers
are concerned. They think
the wolves will kill too much
wildlife and cattle. Other
people say wolves are
important in maintaining a
healthy ecosystem.

What do you think?

WORDS YOU SHOULD KNOW

alpha (AL • fa) — a term used for the leading wolf in a pack

amended (uh • MEN • did) — added to

ancestor (AN • sess • ter) — a grandparent or forebear earlier in history

bounty (BOWN • tee) — a reward or prize

canines (KAY • nynz) — sharp, pointed teeth in the front of the mouth; fangs

carnivore (KAR • nih • vor) — a flesh-eating animal

colonists (KAHL • uh • nists) — people who come from another country to live and work in a place

communicate (kuh • MYOO • nih • kayt) — to pass messages back and forth

continually (kun • TIN • yoo • uh • lee) — over and over again

coyote (kye • OH • tee) — a small animal with reddish fur that looks like a dog

den (DEN) — a warm, safe place such as a hole in the ground or a cave where an animal can rest or give birth to young

ecosystem (EK • oh • siss • tim) — all the plants and animals living and interacting in a certain area

expression (ex • PRESH • un) — a look on the face that shows feelings or meaning

extinct (ex • TINKT) — no longer living

harmonize (HAR • mo • nyz) — to sing different notes together

jackal (JACK • il) — an animal that looks like a dog

mammal (MAM • il) — one of a group of warm-blooded animals that have hair and nurse their young with milk

pant (PANT) — to take short, quick breaths with the mouth open

pelt (PELT) — the skin with the fur left on

population (pop • yoo • LAY • shun) — the number of animals of a certain kind that are present in an area

predator (PREH • di • ter) — an animal that kills and eats other animals

prey (PRAY) — animals that are killed by predators

social (SO • shil) — living in groups rather than alone

species (SPEE • ceez) — a group of plants or animals that are alike in certain ways

territory (TAIR • ih • tor • ee) — area of land that an animal or a group of animals regards as their own

tundra (TUHN • dra) — land in a cold climate that has no trees and that is frozen most of the year

weaned (WEEND) — no longer drinking mother's milk

wilderness (WIL • der • ness) — wild areas far from towns and settlements

INDEX

About the Author

Emilie Utteg Lepthien earned a BS and an MA degree and a certificate in school administration from Northwestern University. She taught third grade, upper grade science and social studies, and was a supervisor and principal of Wicker Park School for twenty years. Mrs. Lepthien has also written and narrated science and social studies scripts for the Radio Council (WBEZ) of the Chicago Board of Education.

Mrs. Lepthien was awarded the American Educator's Medal by Freedoms Foundation. She is a member of Delta Kappa Gamma Society International, Illinois Women's Press Association, National Federation of Press Women, Iota Sigma Epsilon journalism sorority, Chicago Principals Association, and is active in church work. She has coauthored primary social studies books for Rand, McNally and Company and served as educational consultant for Encyclopaedia Britannica Films.